CONTINENTS

ANTARCTICA

by Maurene J. Hinds

Author, The ... tant
... othe
... very,
and Advent... gion

CORE
LIBRARY

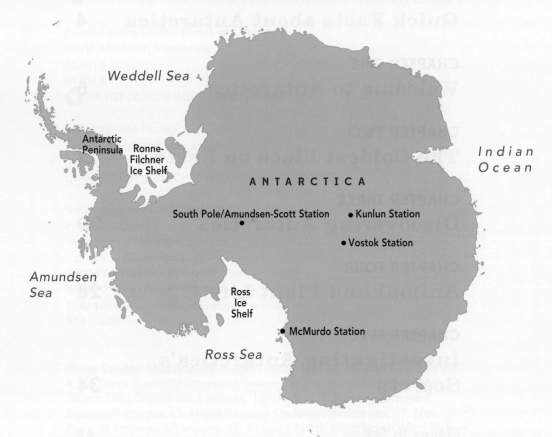

Weddell Sea

Antarctic
Peninsula

Ronne-
Filchner
Ice Shelf

A N T A R C T I C A

Indian
Ocean

South Pole/Amundsen-Scott Station ● ● Kunlun Station

● Vostok Station

Amundsen
Sea

Ross
Ice
Shelf

McMurdo Station ●

Ross Sea

South Pacific
Ocean

QUICK FACTS ABOUT ANTARCTICA

- **Highest point:** Vinson Massif, 16,066 feet (4,897 m)

- **Area:** The Antarctic continent is about 5.5 million square miles (14 million sq km) in area. In winter, however, the oceans surrounding the continent freeze. This increases its area by a great deal.

- **Widest distance across:** About 3,106 miles (4,999 km)

- **Key industries:** Scientific research and tourism are the only human activities in Antarctica. Some offshore fishing is permitted.

- **Population:** No permanent residents live in Antarctica. About 4,000 scientists live at more than 40 research stations across the continent during the summer, and about 1,000 brave the brutal winter.

- **Largest research station:** McMurdo Station

- **Number of countries:** Twenty-nine countries operate research bases in Antarctica. No single country owns Antarctica.

CHAPTER ONE

WELCOME TO ANTARCTICA!

Antarctica is covered in ice year-round. It may seem as though almost nothing could live in such a climate. Most of its residents are animals that are well suited to the extreme cold.

No humans live on Antarctica permanently. No indigenous, or native, people have ever lived in the region. But humans do visit Antarctica. Scientists live

Gentoo penguins have evolved to survive in Antarctica's harsh landscape.

at research bases for a few months to a year. Tourists also visit during the summer months.

An Extreme Landscape

Traveling in Antarctica can be dangerous. The temperatures are extreme. So is the landscape. There are huge ice shelves, icebergs, and glaciers. This makes it hard to reach the mainland. Large cracks in the ice make travel dangerous and difficult.

Antarctica's Firstborn?

Most historians believe the first person born in Antarctica was Emilio Marcos de Palma. He was born in 1978. Because no one country claims Antarctica, de Palma is a citizen of his parents' country, Argentina. He was born near the tip of the Antarctic Peninsula.

Antarctica's landscape features big changes in elevation. Oceans surround the continent. But most of Antarctica is well above sea level. This is because of the thick ice that covers it.

Antarctica is big. The continent is almost 1.5 times the size of the United States. The areas

Travel can be difficult and dangerous in Antarctica's ever-changing landscape of glaciers, icebergs, and ice shelves.

that do not melt in summer measure about 5.5 million square miles (14 million sq km). When the sea freezes during winter, it almost doubles the size of Antarctica.

Antarctica averages only about two inches (5 cm) of precipitation per year. This is because of the region's dry air and cold temperatures. The coldest temperature ever recorded on Earth, -129 degrees Fahrenheit (-89°C), was recorded at Antarctica's Vostok Station. Temperatures in the warmest areas of the continent can reach almost 60 degrees Fahrenheit (16°C) during summer. The average temperature at the South Pole is -58 degrees Fahrenheit (-50°C).

CHAPTER TWO

THE COLDEST PLACE ON EARTH

Antarctica is a place where ice covers almost everything much of the time. This ice is constantly moving and shifting. Glaciers cover much of the continent. Glaciers are like slow-moving rivers of ice. Because the ice of Antarctica is constantly moving, the geographic location of the South Pole has to be marked again every year.

Tourists enjoy the beautiful but intimidating landscape of Paradise Bay.

Named the Antarctic Peninsula, this area is next to one of the larger ice shelves, the Ronne-Filchner Ice Shelf.

The Ellsworth Mountains are on the western side of Antarctica. Vinson Massif, the highest point in Antarctica, is part of this range. The Amundsen and Ross Seas are both west of the Transantarctic Mountains. The Ross Ice Shelf, the largest ice shelf in Antarctica, is also there. It is about the same size as France.

Katabatic Winds

Katabatic winds carry air from a higher elevation down a slope under the force of gravity. These winds can rush down slopes at speeds of up to 66 feet per second (20 m/sec). They often blow out from Antarctica's large, elevated ice sheets. These high-speed winds also lead to the creation of ventifacts. These are unusual rock formations caused by windblown sand and ice.

The Eastern Region

Most of Antarctica is on the eastern side of the Transantarctic Mountains. This side of the continent includes the Amundsen-Scott South Pole Station,

A wing-mounted camera on NASA's DC-8 flying laboratory plane captured this image of Vinson Massif, the tallest peak in Antarctica.

the Kunlun Station, and the Vostok Station. The eastern side of Antarctica is also home to the thickest ice on Earth. It is almost three miles (4.5 km) thick at the thickest point.

Islands and Volcanoes

Many islands surround Antarctica. As the seasons change, the water surrounding Antarctica freezes and thaws each year. When this water freezes, it

CHAPTER THREE

DISCOVERING ANTARCTICA

People began to explore Antarctica during the early 1800s. No one is certain who first landed in Antarctica. But many believe it was US seal hunter Captain John Davis in 1821. British sealer James Weddell reached Antarctica in 1822. During this expedition, Weddell traveled farther south than anyone had before him.

Two members of Sir Ernest Shackleton's 1907–08 expedition at work in the group's winter hut

Early Beliefs about Antarctica

Ancient Greek philosophers believed that a great continent existed in the Southern Hemisphere. This was before people had explored Antarctica. The Roman mathematician, astronomer, and geographer Ptolemy held the same belief. He included a vast *Terra Australis*, or "Southern Land," in his maps of the world. For the next 1,500 years, mapmakers included a large southern landmass on their maps even though they had no information about it. People believed this unknown continent was populated with strange people. They thought it could someday be settled.

Early Exploration

In 1841 James Clark Ross, a British naval officer, explored the Victoria Barrier. This area was later renamed the Ross Ice Shelf in his honor. In the following years, he explored the areas now known as James Ross Island, Snow Hill Island, and Seymour Island.

Little was known about Antarctica until the early 1900s. From 1901 to 1904, British explorer Robert Falcon Scott led a team of explorers on an expedition to Antarctica.

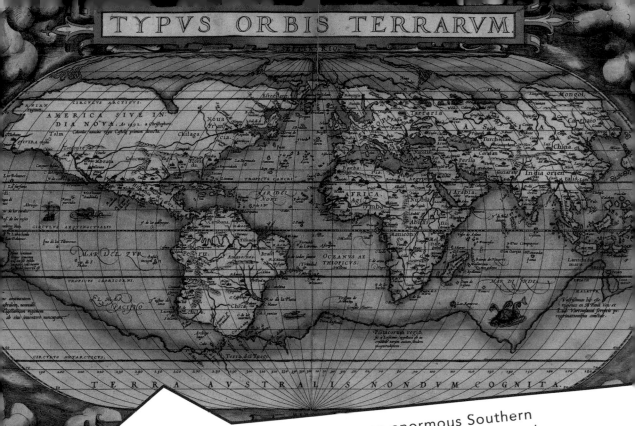

This world map from 1570 shows an enormous Southern Land, which ancient civilizations believed was populated by strange people.

One of the men on this team was the famous explorer Sir Ernest Shackleton.

Scott tried to reach the South Pole a few years later. But Roald Amundsen, a Norwegian, reached the pole first on December 14, 1911. Scott and his team reached the South Pole shortly after, on January 17, 1912. Scott and his four companions died during their return trip.

Two sailing ships search for a place to make landfall along the ice barrier of the Antarctic coast during the 1800s.

Antarctica Today

Many parts of Antarctica are named after early explorers. These include the Weddell, Ross, Davis, and Amundsen Seas. Ice shelves sport names such as Ross and Shackleton.

The first Antarctic explorers traveled on foot and with sleds and dogs. Today people use airplanes and helicopters. Buildings in Antarctica today are much stronger than the huts used by the first explorers. But life is still dangerous in Antarctica. Bringing in supplies is a challenge. During the summer, people bring supplies to the South Pole on the McMurdo Highway using large snow machines. The trip takes four weeks. During the winter, conditions make it too

Sir Ernest Shackleton

In 1914 Sir Ernest Shackleton and his team set out to cross the entire continent of Antarctica. Shackleton had wanted to be the first to reach the South Pole. He tried twice, but he was unable to do so. This time he planned to travel across the South Pole. Shackleton's ship, the *Endurance*, became trapped in the ice. The entire team was stranded for months. In April 1916, Shackleton and five others took a small boat and sailed for help. They later returned to rescue those left behind. Remarkably, the entire team survived. They became famous for their determination.

CHAPTER FOUR

ANIMAL AND PLANT LIFE

I t is hard to believe that anything can live in Antarctica. But scientists have discovered that a fascinating range of life forms make their homes in the coldest place on Earth.

Marine Mammals

The ocean surrounding Antarctica is full of life. Some animals visit only during the warmer summer months. Others live there year-round.

Crabeater seals, which live in Antarctica's pack ice, are the most abundant seals in the world.

Humpback whales are between 39 and 52 feet (12 to 16 m) long and weigh about 79,000 pounds (36,000 kg).

Like all whales in the Antarctic, minke whales have a protective layer of blubber that allows them to survive in icy water. Humpback whales travel long distances to feed in the Antarctic during the summer. Several other species of whales also live part of the time in the Southern Ocean.

Dolphins and porpoises also spend time in the waters of the Southern Ocean. Orcas, also known as killer whales, are actually the largest species of dolphin. Orcas are skilled hunters. They work together to catch their prey. This includes penguins, fish, seals, and whales.

Crabeater seals live around the Antarctic Peninsula and in the Ross Sea. Leopard and Weddell seals live throughout the ocean surrounding Antarctica. Weddell seals live farther south than any other mammals on Earth. Ross seals live in the pack ice near the Ross and Ronne-Filchner Ice Shelves. Pack ice is the name for large areas of ice floating close together in the ocean.

Land and Air Animals

Many sea birds live in Antarctica. Most live there only during the summer months. Sea birds called albatross live on the

Microscopic Life Forms

Antarctica is home to hundreds of subglacial lakes, which lie underneath the continent's ice sheets. Scientists have found evidence of microbial life in Lake Vostok and Lake Untersee, two subglacial lakes. These bacteria have been isolated, or kept separate, from all other forms of bacteria for millions of years. Yet they are similar to other kinds of bacteria. Knowing that these bacteria can survive under such difficult conditions made the scientists believe bacteria might be able to exist under similar conditions on other planets.

CHAPTER FIVE

INVESTIGATING ANTARCTICA'S SECRETS

Research in Antarctica has provided scientists with clues about many issues. This includes the way in which human activity is affecting our planet.

Antarctica has the cleanest air on Earth. This is because there is very little human activity there. Researchers study Antarctic air to learn more about Earth's atmosphere.

The cramped living quarters inside the old geodesic dome at the South Pole Station had sleeping space for only 33 people.

Studying the Ozone Layer

One area of study is the ozone layer. The ozone layer is part of the atmosphere that surrounds the earth. The ozone layer protects our planet from the harmful rays of the sun. Scientists discovered a hole in the ozone layer over Antarctica in 1985. As researchers learn more about this hole and the ozone layer in general, they can also learn more about how human activity and other factors are affecting our planet.

Aurora Australis

An aurora is a natural display of light in the sky. They are caused by particles and radiation from the sun colliding with the earth's magnetic fields. These displays happen most frequently in the polar regions. Many people are familiar with the northern lights, or aurora borealis. In the southern hemisphere, these light are called aurora australis, or the southern lights. People can see these lights from the southernmost parts of South America, New Zealand, and Australia.

Secrets in the Ice

Antarctica holds much of one of Earth's greatest resources, water. Ninety percent of all ice on the

Members of Japan's Antarctic research team use weather balloons to study aspects of global climate change.

planet is located in the southernmost continent. If all of this ice were to melt, researchers believe it would raise the sea level by 260 feet (79 m).

research center through the winter. The structure is designed to withstand high winds and extreme cold. It even has a greenhouse to grow fruits and vegetables.

Robot Helpers

People are now able to access more parts of Antarctica than ever before. But there are still places too dangerous for scientists to go. Robots allow researchers to gather information from areas humans can't reach. One project uses robots to create three-dimensional images of areas under the Antarctic ice. Scientists also use robots to film and collect information underwater. Robotic unmanned submarines explore the waters deep below ice shelves. There are also robotic unmanned aircraft that fly low over vast ice sheets to collect data.

Cooperation

Thanks to the Antarctic Treaty, many nations work together to protect Antarctica's environment and wildlife. Scientific bases and research centers do their best to recycle or remove their waste. Researchers also take care not to damage the areas they visit.

The Antarctic Treaty also ensures that commercial activities are kept to a minimum on the continent. Commercial activities are activities meant to earn money. While tourism is allowed in Antarctica, industries such as mining are not. Some limited commercial fishing is permitted offshore.

Antarctica is an example of people working together peacefully to learn more about our planet, its past, and its future. There is much to study and learn in Antarctica.

EXPLORE ONLINE

One of the subjects of Chapter Five is the hole in the ozone layer that scientists discovered over Antarctica. The Web site below also provides information about the ozone layer. As you know, every source is different. How is the information given on this Web site different from the information in this chapter? What information is the same? How do the two sources present information differently? What can you learn from this Web site?

The Ozone Layer
www.mycorelibrary.com/antarctica